ALEXANDER
HAMILTON

THE STORY OF A STATESMAN

ALEXANDER HAMILTON

THE STORY OF A STATESMAN

HEATHER E. SCHWARTZ

LERNER PUBLICATIONS ◆ MINNEAPOLIS

Lerner Publications Company
An imprint of Lerner Publishing Group, Inc.
241 First Avenue North
Minneapolis, MN 55401 USA

For reading levels and more information, look up this title at www.lernerbooks.com.

Image credits: Wikimedia Commons (public domain), pp. 2, 34, 35, 36; Litererian1912/Wikimedia Commons (CC BY-SA 4.0), p. 6; Library of Congress, pp. 8, 9, 25, 27; National Archives, pp. 10, 22, 29; Print Collector/Hulton Archive/Getty Images, p. 11; The Miriam and Ira D. Wallach Division of Art, Prints and Photographs: Print Collection, The New York Public Library, pp. 12, 20, 33; Culture Club/ Hulton Archive/Getty Images, p. 13; duncan1890/DigitalVision Vectors/Getty Images, p. 15; Architect of the Capitol, pp. 16, 21; Courtesy of the Museum of the City of New York, image courtesy of The Athenaeum/Wikimedia Commons, p. 17; Universal Images Group/Getty Images, p. 18; U.S. Army Center of Military History, p. 19; Gift of Mr. and Mrs. George W. Davison/National Gallery of Art, Washington DC, p. 23; Gift of Edgar William and Bernice Chrysler Garbisch, 1963/Metropolitan Museum of Art, p. 24; traveler1116/iStock/Getty Images, p. 26; MPI/Archive Photos/Getty Images, p. 28 (top); Internet Archive Book Images/Wikimedia Commons, pp. 28 (bottom), 39; Francis Miller/The LIFE Picture Collection/Getty Images, p. 30; Beinecke Rare Book & Manuscript Library, Yale University/Wikimedia Commons, p. 31; Hulton Archive/Getty Images, p. 32; Bettmann/Getty Images, p. 37; The New York Historical Society/ Archive Photos/Getty Images, p. 38; Chip Somodevilla/Getty Images, p. 40; Gladys Vega/Getty Images, p. 41. Cover: The Bureau of Engraving and Printing/Wikimedia Commons (public domain); billnoll/E+/Getty Images (background).

Main body text set in Rotis Serif Std. Typeface provided by Adobe Systems.

Library of Congress Cataloging-in-Publication Data

Names: Schwartz, Heather E., author.
Title: Alexander Hamilton : the story of a statesman / by Heather E. Schwartz.
Other titles: Story of a statesman
Description: Minneapolis : Lerner Publications, [2020] | Series: Gateway biographies | Includes
    bibliographical references and index. | Audience: Ages 9–14 | Audience: Grades 4–6 | Summary: "A
    founder of the country turned cultural phenomenon, Alexander Hamilton helped create American
    democracy. Follow his story as an orphaned immigrant to successful statesman."– Provided by
    publisher.
Identifiers: LCCN 2019030777 (print) | LCCN 2019030778 (ebook) | ISBN 9781541577480 (library binding)
    | ISBN 9781541588868 (paperback) | ISBN 9781541583047 (ebook)
Subjects: LCSH: Hamilton, Alexander, 1757–1804–Juvenile literature. | Statesmen–United States–
    Biography–Juvenile literature. | United States–History–Revolution, 1775–1783–Juvenile literature. |
    United States–Politics and government–1783–1809–Juvenile literature.
Classification: LCC E302.6.H2 S267 2020 (print) | LCC E302.6.H2 (ebook) | DDC 973.4092 [B]–dc23

LC record available at https://lccn.loc.gov/2019030777
LC ebook record available at https://lccn.loc.gov/2019030778

Manufactured in the United States of America
1-46771-47762-9/23/2019

CONTENTS

PORTRAIT OF ALEXANDER HAMILTON IN 1794

On a dark night in 1781, Alexander Hamilton prepared his troops for battle. The plan was simple but daring. Silently, with their muskets unloaded, they would sneak up on the British soldiers occupying Yorktown, Virginia. Instead of firing guns and alerting their target, Hamilton ordered his men to keep silent, relying only on bayonets to do their work. Their goal: a quick victory with few casualties.

In collaboration with French troops fighting for the same cause—America's freedom—Hamilton led his men to move in on the British. Once detected, they dodged bullets and grenades from the enemy. But the British proved no match for the Americans in brutal hand-to-hand combat.

Within ten minutes, the British had surrendered and the Battle of Yorktown was over. Only nine Americans had been killed. For Hamilton, the victory was both historic and personal. The win was a turning point in the Revolutionary War (1775–1783) and secured his reputation

CARTE DE L'ISLE DE NIEVES

NEVIS IS LOCATED IN THE CARIBBEAN SEA.

as a courageous war hero. It set him on a path he couldn't even dream of as a child, positioning him for glory as a founder of an entirely new nation.

YOUNG ALEXANDER

Alexander Hamilton began his life on a tiny island called Nevis in the British West Indies. Records of his exact birthdate aren't clear, but historians believe he was born on January 11, in either 1755 or 1757.

Growing up, Alexander was bullied because he didn't have a traditional family. His mother, Rachel Fawcett, had been married before, to an abusive man. She ran away from him, leaving her son Peter behind on Saint Croix, another island. When she met James Hamilton, the couple couldn't marry because Fawcett could not get divorced. Divorces were uncommon then and very challenging. They lived together anyway and had two children, James and Alexander. Because their parents weren't married, Alexander and his brother were considered illegitimate.

The family was poor, and Alexander's illegitimate status meant he wasn't allowed to attend the school run by the Church of England. He managed to get some education at a Jewish school and from private tutors when his parents could afford them. When he was ten, the family moved back to Saint Croix. Soon after, his father abandoned them. Fawcett supported them by finding a house where they could live upstairs and run a shop on the ground floor.

The Hamilton family was managing, but soon tragedy struck. Fawcett became ill with a fever and died. Her first husband made sure that Peter inherited his mother's entire estate. Orphaned and destitute, Alexander and James went to live with a cousin. When the cousin died, Alexander and his brother were again left with nothing.

ALEXANDER FACED A LOT OF HARDSHIPS GROWING UP.

HAMILTON'S BIRTH YEAR

Historians have never been able to determine Hamilton's exact birth year. Documentation from the time offers conflicting information. Hamilton himself wanted people to believe he was born in 1757. But a court document says he was thirteen in 1768, putting his birth year two years earlier, in 1755. Historians believe Hamilton authored a poem published in 1771. The poem was sent to a newspaper with a note from the author, who claimed to be about seventeen years old. It was signed with the initials A.H. If Hamilton did write the note and poem, that would put his birth year at 1754.

It is possible Hamilton lied about his age. He may have wanted people to believe he was younger in order to get a position as an apprentice. A younger age would also have made his accomplishments appear even more extraordinary.

REGARDLESS OF HIS AGE, MANY PEOPLE ARE AMAZED BY HAMILTON'S ACCOMPLISHMENTS.

Alexander started to support himself. James did the same, working as a carpenter. At about fourteen years old, Alexander was working for a respected merchant. When his boss left the island, he gave Alexander the responsibility of running the business. It was a vote of confidence in Alexander's ability, and Alexander enjoyed the work. He learned to take charge and command other workers. But Alexander wanted to leave the island too. He wanted more education and longed to see the British colonies. Neither seemed likely to happen. Though he was working, he was still poor. And nothing could change his status as illegitimate.

Hamilton was a talented writer and had strong opinions. After a severe hurricane, he wrote a letter to his father. The letter fell into the hands of minister and journalist Hugh Knox. Knox was impressed with Hamilton's letter and had it published in a newspaper called the *Royal Danish American Gazette*. Hamilton

ALEXANDER'S LETTER ABOUT THE HURRICANE APPEARED IN A SIMILAR NEWSPAPER.

wrote, "A great part of the buildings throughout the Island are levelled to the ground, almost all the rest very much shattered . . . whole families running about the streets, unknowing where to find a place of shelter."

People recognized Hamilton's intelligence and talent. They collected money to send him north for schooling. In 1772 he arrived and quickly settled into life in the British colonies. He began attending the Elizabethtown Academy, in New Jersey, and later King's College, in New York. He studied medicine with the goal of becoming a doctor.

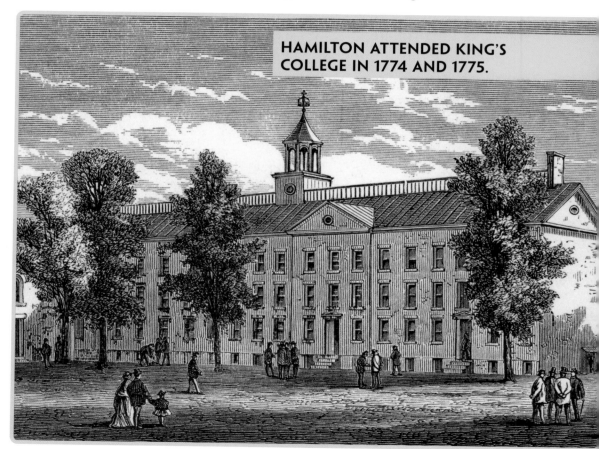

HAMILTON ATTENDED KING'S COLLEGE IN 1774 AND 1775.

THE COLONIES

The British colonies Alexander Hamilton dreamed of in North America included New Hampshire, Massachusetts, Rhode Island, Connecticut, New York, New Jersey, Pennsylvania, Delaware, Maryland, Virginia, North Carolina, South Carolina, and Georgia. By 1772 the colonies were getting restless and people began to take sides.

Loyalists believed the colonies should remain loyal to Britain. Patriots felt the colonies should break away to become an independent nation. In New York, most people supported Britain, including many King's College students and faculty. There were only a few exceptions—and Alexander Hamilton was one of them.

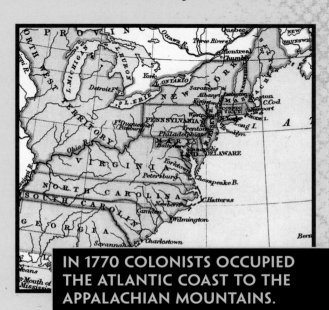

IN 1770 COLONISTS OCCUPIED THE ATLANTIC COAST TO THE APPALACHIAN MOUNTAINS.

MILITARY MAN

By 1775 the Revolutionary War had begun. British troops occupied New York, and King's College closed because of safety concerns. Hamilton's schooling ended abruptly. He knew it was time that he quit just talking about the revolution and joined the fight. He didn't know he was about to jump into a military career and help found a nation.

THE START OF THE REVOLUTION

In the years leading up to the Revolutionary War, Britain needed to pay back debts from the French and Indian War (1754–1763). Britain created laws to collect tax money from the colonies. These included the Stamp Act, passed in 1765, which taxed all printed papers, including newspapers and playing cards, and the Townshend Act, passed in 1767, which taxed essential items, such as paint, glass, and tea. In 1770 the colonists protested violently. Many felt the taxes were unfair because the colonies had no representation in British government.

Britain agreed to repeal most of the taxes. But the tea tax brought in too much money to give up. The Tea Act was passed in 1773 so that Britain could continue collecting the tax from the colonies. In an angry protest, a group of men called the Sons of Liberty went to Boston Harbor to find ships that were carrying tea from China. The Sons of Liberty threw the tea overboard rather than allow it to be unloaded and taxed. This is popularly known as the Boston Tea Party.

Britain passed laws to prevent more rebellion. But the laws only angered many colonists who resented Britain's rule. Tensions kept building, and the Revolutionary War broke out.

The first shots were fired on April 19, 1775, in Lexington and Concord in Massachusetts. In Lexington an argument between the British and colonists started on the town green and became violent. The British quickly retreated. The Battles of Lexington and Concord started when British troops marched from Lexington, intending to take all the weapons from the patriots. Paul Revere and other patriots rode to warn of the invasion, and the city was able to fend off the British too.

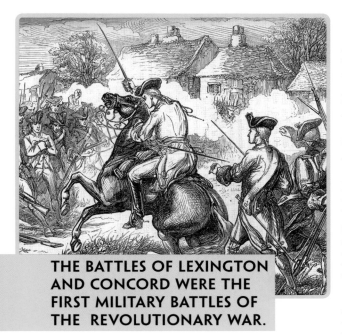

THE BATTLES OF LEXINGTON AND CONCORD WERE THE FIRST MILITARY BATTLES OF THE REVOLUTIONARY WAR.

Only about twenty years old, Hamilton organized his own militia of around twenty-five soldiers. He led them successfully in battle. He didn't have wealth or status, but his strong leadership earned him recognition. In 1776 he accepted a post commanding troops for New York.

Hamilton recruited men to fight the British. His company built Bunker Hill, a strong fort overlooking the city. General George Washington, leader of the patriots, visited and praised them for their work.

After the Declaration of Independence was signed on July 4, 1776, battles in New York grew more intense. The British were frustrated with the colonies' decision to break away. Hamilton continued to lead his militia. Hamilton didn't have many resources and struggled to keep his troops supplied with shoes as the weather grew cold. Despite this, they kept fighting. He moved his troops from New York to New Jersey. They secured Washington's passage to Princeton by firing continuously on the enemy.

HAMILTON WAS BUSY FIGHTING THE WAR AND DID NOT SIGN THE DECLARATION OF INDEPENDENCE.

Washington was impressed and asked his aides and officers about the troops that had made his trip possible. One of them told him, "It was a model of discipline; at their head was a boy, and I wondered at his youth, but what was my surprise when he was pointed out to me as that Hamilton of whom we had already heard so much."

In the Battle of Princeton, in January 1777, some of the last shots fired came from Hamilton's troops. The battle ended in a victory for the colonists. In March, Hamilton was promoted to lieutenant colonel and joined Washington's staff. He became Washington's secretary and confidential aide. The position gave Hamilton opportunities to work with politicians and military officers.

While his political career was taking off, Hamilton was introduced to Elizabeth Schuyler. Schuyler, also known as Betsey or Eliza, was a charity worker with big political ideas. She was the daughter of the Revolutionary War general Philip Schuyler. She and Hamilton bonded over their shared interest in politics and started courting. Schuyler and Hamilton married in December 1780. She would continue to shape Hamilton's political beliefs throughout his career.

MEETING ELIZA

Hamilton and his future wife first met in 1778, when he stayed with her family while traveling as a military officer. Two years later, they met at a party Schuyler's aunt threw for Washington's staff. Though she was from a prominent family and he grew up poor, they bonded quickly. Her family was happy with the match, in part because Hamilton had the same political beliefs as them.

SCHUYLER HAD A PASSION FOR POLITICS.

When Washington took soldiers to Valley Forge, Pennsylvania, in December 1777, Hamilton went with them. He stayed through the six-month encampment, enduring a harsh winter that threatened the soldiers' lives. Later, Hamilton went with Washington to the Battle of Monmouth and had his horse shot from under him. Through it all, Hamilton learned to lead and strengthened his friendship with Washington.

HAMILTON (*RIGHT*) WORKED CLOSELY WITH WASHINGTON.

Still, Hamilton longed to prove himself as a military leader, and he stayed alert for the opportunity. It finally came when a siege at Yorktown, Virginia, was planned. A French lieutenant colonel was set to lead the American troops, but Hamilton wanted the job. He went to Washington and convinced his friend to give him the command.

Hamilton's troops moved silently, sneaking up on their British enemies in the night. Realizing they were surrounded, the British quickly surrendered. Hamilton was hailed as a hero. The Battle of Yorktown was one of the last battles of the Revolutionary War and a deciding factor in the United States' victory.

Victory in Yorktown satisfied Hamilton's ambition for military glory. He left the army shortly after and returned home to Albany, New York. He and Eliza soon welcomed their first son, Philip.

WHILE HAMILTON LED HIS SILENT ATTACK, REVOLUTIONISTS STORMED BRITISH FORTS.

FOUNDER

By 1782 Hamilton had created a new path and a new future for himself. He had risen to a position of power and status as a war hero who served under George Washington. He was appointed to the Congress of the Confederation. This branch of the newly established US government was empowered to declare war, sign treaties, settle disputes between states, and borrow and print money. He served until 1783, helping to draft the peace treaty that ended the Revolutionary War.

After leaving Congress, Hamilton opened a law office in New York City. He was criticized for representing Loyalists who had sided with Britain in the war. But he strongly believed it was time to move on as one united country. He also felt this tactic would benefit the new nation's economy. Loyalist merchants needed to feel welcome doing business in the United States.

Hamilton went on to found the Bank of New York in 1784. In 1787 he began to serve in the New York State Legislature. That same year, he attended the US Constitutional Convention. He fought for the government structure he believed in for the new nation.

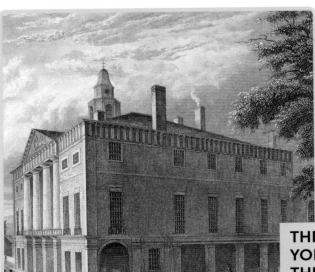

THE FEDERAL HALL IN NEW YORK CITY WAS HOME TO THE FIRST CONGRESS.

Hamilton's strong opinions went against the grain. He thought that the president should be similar to Britain's king and that the upper body of legislation should operate like the British House of Lords. He also believed senators should serve for life. He preferred a government structure that did not include state leadership and had only one political authority: the federal government.

Hamilton's ideal government was considered radical and was not embraced by everyone. But he had other ideas as well. He wanted to create three branches of government: executive, legislative, and judiciary. This idea made it into the new US Constitution, which Hamilton, along with other founders of the country, signed in 1787. Hamilton then used his writing talents to contribute fifty-one essays to the *Federalist Papers*. The papers successfully convinced his home state of New York to ratify the Constitution. The country could begin moving forward under its new laws.

THE *FEDERALIST PAPERS*

In order for the US Constitution to become the law of the land, nine of the country's thirteen states had to ratify, or approve it. Some were against it, feeling the Constitution gave too much power to the federal government and not enough to states. Others were for it, believing that the document would give the federal government the power it needed to keep the Union together.

Founders Alexander Hamilton, James Madison, and John Jay wrote eighty-five letters to newspapers outlining reasons states should approve the Constitution. They signed all of their letters with the pseudonym "Publius." Hamilton wrote the majority of the letters. They became known as the *Federalist Papers*.

HAMILTON SIGNED THE CONSTITUTION IN 1787.

In 1789 George Washington became the first president of the United States. When Congress established the country's Treasury Department, Washington appointed Hamilton the first secretary of the treasury. Hamilton had a lot of work to do in his new position. The new country was saddled with war debt and needed a plan to find its financial footing. Hamilton was determined to pay off the debts. He wanted other countries to view the United States as reliable in case the new nation needed credit in the future.

WASHINGTON SERVED AS PRESIDENT FROM 1789–1797.

First, Hamilton had the federal government take on states' debts, which helped states and encouraged their loyalty. To bring in money, he convinced Congress to approve a whiskey tax and a high import tariff. Hamilton designed these measures to encourage domestic production. He did not want the United States to be dependent on imports from Britain. He also fought to create a national bank. The bank would hold federal funds and manage finances for the government.

THE WHISKEY REBELLION

In 1794 Hamilton was drawn into a different kind of battle. It wasn't purely political. Pennsylvania farmers were unhappy about the high whiskey tax the new federal government had imposed. They relied on the sale and distribution of whiskey to supplement their incomes. When government officers came to collect the tax, angry farmers tarred and feathered them instead. The rebellion gained strength when they burned a tax inspector's home.

The whiskey tax had been Hamilton's idea to pay off war debt. Now, he had to defend it. At Hamilton's urging, Washington used the military to stop what was later dubbed the Whiskey Rebellion. Hamilton commanded the troops, and the farmers gave up quickly. No one was killed in the skirmish.

The success set a precedent for the country. Troops could cross state lines, and the federal government could call upon the military to uphold the law.

WASHINGTON CALLS TROOPS TO STOP THE REBELLION.

In 1789 war broke out in France. The French had helped the colonies break free from British rule. Now they were fighting against their king. The French Revolution offered a decision between fighting for freedom abroad or strengthening the United States' new government. Hamilton was up to the task. Given the country's debt and brand-new government, he convinced Washington that the United States should remain neutral in the French affair. The president issued the Neutrality Proclamation in 1793.

Despite the proclamation, a French ambassador began recruiting Americans to fight for France. Then Britain got involved and started to impress, or force, Americans into service for Britain. The Revolutionary War had just ended. But it seemed the United States might go to war with Britain again.

THE US DECIDED NOT TO FIGHT IN THE FRENCH REVOLUTION.

Hamilton's solution was a treaty that would stop Britain in its tracks. He wanted Britain to agree to stop impressing Americans into service and seizing US ships. He also wanted to remove British forts from US soil. Hamilton didn't get the treaty he wanted, but Jay's Treaty, as it was called, put an end to the threat of war.

HAMILTON (*SECOND FROM RIGHT*) WITH WASHINGTON AND THE REST OF HIS PRESIDENTIAL CABINET

POLITICAL OPPONENTS

Hamilton worked to do what he felt was best for the United States. But he was challenged by the other founders, who had different ideas. Secretary of State Thomas Jefferson was against the idea of creating a national bank. He and his supporters said it was unconstitutional because nothing in the new US Constitution allowed it. Hamilton and his allies, on the other hand, argued the US Constitution did not forbid the establishment of a national bank, which meant it was constitutional.

In 1791 Washington approved the plan, establishing the Bank of the United States. Hamilton's work as secretary of the treasury strengthened the country financially. It also led to the emergence of two new political parties. Hamilton led the Federalists, and Jefferson led the Democratic-Republicans.

Hamilton and Jefferson were soon battling over other ideological differences. Hamilton believed that the United States should focus its economy on manufacturing instead of agriculture. Jefferson disagreed. The argument erupted into a full-blown fight as each side wrote out their positions in national newspapers.

JEFFERSON BECAME HAMILTON'S POLITICAL OPPONENT.

Some battles were easier to win than others. In the early days of the United States, Hamilton was concerned about the new country's currency system. People across the country were using different kinds of money printed by individual states and banks. When Hamilton pushed for a national currency, no one argued against him.

The Mint Act was passed in 1792. It established the United States Mint, the only manufacturer allowed to print and circulate US money.

Still, Hamilton was growing discouraged by the attacks from his political foes. His position as secretary of the treasury was high in status but low in pay. These were reasons enough to resign. But there was another reason too. Hamilton was involved in a scandal.

HAMILTON FOUNDED
THE BANK OF THE
UNITED STATES.

SCANDAL AND DISAPPOINTMENT

In 1791 Hamilton did something that would haunt him for the rest of his political career. He began an extramarital affair with a woman named Maria Reynolds. In early 1792, her husband, James, demanded money from Hamilton, threatening to expose the affair. Hamilton paid him $1,000, equal to about $25,000 today. He continued the affair and paid even more to satisfy Reynolds's additional demands.

A few months later, Reynolds and some other men were arrested and charged with a crime that involved swindling Revolutionary War veterans. One of the men claimed that Hamilton was involved too. When the crime was investigated, it became clear that Hamilton was not a part of it. But during the investigation, Hamilton confessed to the affair in great detail. Word spread quickly to other leaders in government, including Jefferson.

HAMILTON WAS ACCUSED OF STEALING MONEY FROM WAR VETERANS.

Hamilton knew his enemies could end his career. He had no chance of ever running a successful political campaign with the scandal on his record. In 1795 he resigned as secretary of the treasury. But his political career wasn't over. The following year, he helped draft Washington's farewell address when the president decided against running for a third term. The address encouraged the country to avoid dividing along party lines and stay out of European conflicts. Many of the ideas presented may have come from Hamilton himself.

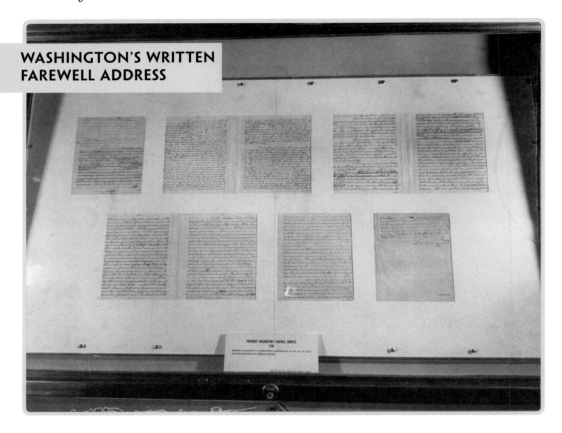

WASHINGTON'S WRITTEN FAREWELL ADDRESS

By late 1796, word of Hamilton's affair was beginning to leak. A journalist learned about the affair from Congressman James Monroe. The journalist falsely accused Hamilton of using government money to pay Reynolds. This sparked a heated argument between Hamilton and Monroe. Hamilton accused Monroe of giving the journalist his personal information. Senator Aaron Burr stepped in to negotiate and prevent a duel.

Realizing his secret was out, Hamilton decided to take control of the situation. He published the *Reynolds Pamphlet*, which offered the truth and details about the affair and payments. While their marriage had hardships, Eliza and Hamilton remained close. She demanded Monroe apologize for lying about Hamilton using government money. Meanwhile, the couple continued their life together. By then, they had several children. Hamilton was contrite and felt a renewed dedication to them. He called Eliza the "best of wives and best of women."

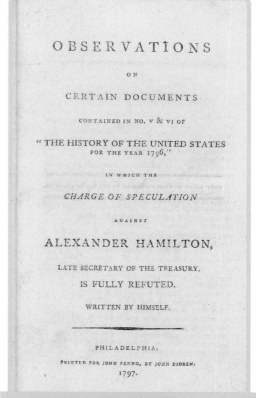

OBSERVATIONS

ON

CERTAIN DOCUMENTS

CONTAINED IN NO. V & VI OF

" THE HISTORY OF THE UNITED STATES FOR THE YEAR 1796,"

IN WHICH THE

CHARGE OF SPECULATION

AGAINST

ALEXANDER HAMILTON,

LATE SECRETARY OF THE TREASURY,

IS FULLY REFUTED.

WRITTEN BY HIMSELF.

PHILADELPHIA:

PRINTED FOR JOHN FENNO, BY JOHN BIOREN.

1797.

HAMILTON DESCRIBED HIS AFFAIR AND CLEARED FALSE ACCUSATIONS IN THE *REYNOLDS PAMPHLET*.

The situation marked another first for the United States government. Hamilton's scandal set the stage for reactions to future leaders' indiscretions. It created the standard for the ways leaders' inappropriate actions would be denounced, accepted, or disregarded for decades to come.

Hamilton's career continued, with a high point in 1798. The country's second president, Federalist John Adams, had asked George Washington to return to government to lead the US military. Washington wanted Hamilton as his second-in-command. Adams disagreed with this decision, but Washington was clear. "I know not where a more competent choice could be made," he said.

Hamilton looked forward to returning to the battlefield as a high-ranking officer. He would be a major general, leading troops in a fight against France. But in the end, his excitement turned to disappointment. Adams negotiated a peace treaty that prevented the looming war.

In 1799 Hamilton suffered another loss when his longtime friend Washington died. He left his position and returned to New York City to practice law. But he remained involved in politics. He was unhappy with the candidates running for president in the 1800 election. They included his political enemy Thomas Jefferson, incumbent John Adams, and Senator Aaron Burr.

PINCKNEY AND HAMILTON BOTH SERVED AS AIDES TO WASHINGTON.

Hamilton worked hard to manipulate what would happen next. He campaigned for Charles Pinckney, a Federalist who could challenge Adams, and distributed a pamphlet in which he attacked the current president's conduct and character. As a result, Jefferson and Burr tied in the election for president. The decision was up to the House of Representatives.

Burr was a Federalist and Jefferson was a Democratic-Republican and an old enemy. But of the two, Hamilton supported Jefferson. Burr had defeated Hamilton's father-in-law in a race for the US Senate years earlier. Hamilton believed Burr had selfish ambitions. "At least Jefferson was honest," Hamilton said in defending his choice.

ELECTING THE PRESIDENT

In modern presidential elections, the presidential candidate chooses a vice presidential running mate. These two candidates represent the same party and run together. When the country was founded, elections were run differently. Candidates ran for president alone. The candidate who received the most votes became president. The runner-up became vice president. This continued until 1804 when the Twelfth Amendment passed and required candidates to have running mates

JEFFERSON SERVED AS
PRESIDENT FROM 1801–1809.

Hamilton helped convince the House to choose Jefferson as the country's third president. This made Burr vice president. Serving under Jefferson, Burr never had the power he wanted. His dreams were dashed, and he blamed Hamilton.

A FINAL DUEL

In 1801 Hamilton's oldest son, Philip, got into an argument with a classmate at Columbia University in New York City. The classmate favored Burr,

BURR BLAMED HAMILTON FOR LOSING HIS PRESIDENTIAL BID.

while Philip Hamilton defended his father's honor. When they couldn't settle their differences verbally, they agreed to a duel.

Duels were illegal in New York. But they were a standing tradition in the US at that time. They were an opportunity to settle differences and defend personal honor. The two opponents would meet with matched weapons and fight.

Philip Hamilton was killed by his classmate's bullet. He died near Weehawken, New Jersey, at just nineteen years old. Alexander Hamilton was crushed.

Three years later, in 1804, Hamilton had another opportunity to thwart Burr's political ambitions. Burr was seeking election as governor of New York. Hamilton did everything he could to make sure Burr would lose. Hamilton's motives were not just personal. He was doing what he felt was right for the United States. He had heard Burr might help the northern states secede from the Union if elected governor.

Hamilton published essays against Burr. At one point, a newspaper published a letter that said he had insulted Burr at a private party. When Burr lost the election, he was sure Hamilton was to blame.

HAMILTON CONTINUED TO FIGHT WITH BURR.

By then, Hamilton no longer had the kind of influence that could alter an election. But Burr demanded an apology regarding the incident at the private party. Hamilton claimed he didn't remember saying anything and refused. As the argument continued, letters between the two flew back and forth.

Friends tried to intervene and ease the building tension. But it was clear that Hamilton and Burr couldn't resolve their differences.

Burr challenged Hamilton to a duel. The date was set for July 11, 1804. Hamilton had led troops and served in the military directly under George Washington. But historians believe he may not have fired a pistol since the Revolutionary War. He was likely out of practice, but he couldn't refuse or back out of the duel.

The night before, Hamilton wrote a letter that indicated his intentions. He planned to miss Burr on his first shot and possibly even his second. "I have resolved, if our [duel] is conducted in the usual manner, and it pleases God to give me the opportunity, to reserve and throw away my first fire, and I have thoughts even of reserving my second fire," he wrote.

HAMILTON AND BURR PREPARE TO DUEL.

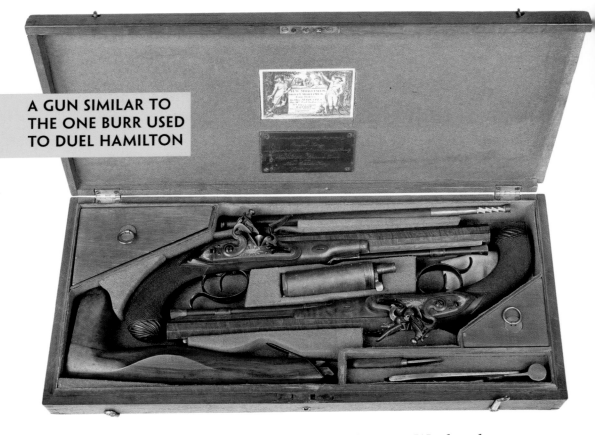

A GUN SIMILAR TO
THE ONE BURR USED
TO DUEL HAMILTON

The pair met at the dueling grounds near Weehawken, New Jersey, where Hamilton's son had died three years earlier. It was seven in the morning. They brought their pistols and their "seconds," people who would fight in their place if they could not continue. Seconds would also make sure the rules were followed. Hamilton's second was his friend Nathaniel Pendleton.

Pendleton recited the rules of dueling. When both men were ready, he shouted, "Fire!" As the two faced off against each other, Hamilton asked for a moment to put on his glasses. By some accounts, Hamilton then fired and missed. By others, Burr was simply quicker to fire first. Some accounts claim Hamilton aimed into the sky with his first shot, indicating he wanted to end the duel. Some say that losing his son made him not want to shoot Burr. Either way, he didn't hit Burr.

But when Burr fired at Hamilton, he hit his mark. A bullet tore through Hamilton's stomach. Burr was led away from Hamilton, and Hamilton was whisked to his home in New York.

New Jersey issued a warrant for Burr, charging him with murder. New York also issued a warrant, but only charged him with a misdemeanor for dueling illegally. In the end, Burr was never tried, but the public was outraged. The incident ruined his political career.

BURR FIRING AT HAMILTON

For Hamilton, the outcome was even worse. After the duel, he knew his injuries were fatal. He spent his last hours surrounded by his family. He was buried in the Trinity Churchyard Cemetery, in Manhattan. He was survived by his wife, Eliza Hamilton, who lived another fifty years, and six of their eight children. Eliza would preserve his legacy by keeping his letters and papers.

Born with many disadvantages, Hamilton managed to carve his own path. He found a way into powerful positions that would determine the direction of a new nation. His life set the tone for a country that believes in hard work, individual grit, and independence. Hamilton's legacy has lived on for centuries as one of the United States' founders.

HAMILTON'S GRIT AND COURAGE HELPED SHAPE THE US.

HAMILTON, THE MUSICAL

In 2008 an American playwright and composer named Lin-Manuel Miranda read a biography called *Alexander Hamilton* by Ron Chernow. He was moved and inspired by the story of a man who rose from nothing to become one of the United States' founders. He quickly got to work writing songs about Hamilton for a project he called *The Hamilton Mixtape*.

Over time, his project transformed to become a full-length musical. *Hamilton* opened on Broadway in 2015. The celebration of Alexander Hamilton's life won several Tony Awards and inspired people all over the country and around the world. It began with Hamilton's childhood in Nevis and ended with the duel, celebrating him as a heroic American figure.

MIRANDA (*CENTER*) PERFORMS IN HIS BROADWAY HIT, *HAMILTON*.

IMPORTANT DATES

1755 OR 1757	ALEXANDER HAMILTON IS BORN ON JANUARY 11.
1772	HE ARRIVES IN THE BRITISH COLONIES.
1775	THE REVOLUTIONARY WAR BEGINS.
1776	THE DECLARATION OF INDEPENDENCE IS SIGNED ON JULY 4.
1777	THE BATTLE OF PRINCETON IS FOUGHT.
1781	THE BATTLE OF YORKTOWN IS THE LAST MAJOR BATTLE OF THE REVOLUTIONARY WAR.
1784	HAMILTON FOUNDS THE BANK OF NEW YORK.
1787	HE SIGNS THE US CONSTITUTION.
1789	GEORGE WASHINGTON BECOMES PRESIDENT.
1789	HAMILTON BECOMES SECRETARY OF THE TREASURY.

1789	THE FRENCH REVOLUTION BEGINS.
1791	THE BANK OF THE UNITED STATES IS ESTABLISHED.
1792	THE MINT ACT IS PASSED.
1794	THE WHISKEY REBELLION TAKES PLACE IN MASSACHUSETTS.
1795	HAMILTON RESIGNS AS SECRETARY OF THE TREASURY.
1801	HAMILTON'S OLDEST SON, PHILIP, IS KILLED IN A DUEL.
1804	HAMILTON DIES IN A DUEL WITH AARON BURR.

SOURCE NOTES

12 "From Alexander Hamilton to the *Royal Danish American Gazette*, 6 September 1772," Columbia University Press, https:// founders.archives.gov/documents/Hamilton/01-01-02-0042.

16 Willard Sterne Randall, "Hamilton Takes Command," *Smithsonian*, January 2003. https://www.smithsonianmag.com/ history/hamilton-takes-command-74722445/.

31 "Alexander Hamilton," New World Encyclopedia, https://www .newworldencyclopedia.org/entry/Alexander_Hamilton.

32 Kieran J. O'Keefe, "Alexander Hamilton," George Washington University, https://www.mountvernon.org/library/digitalhistory /digital-encyclopedia/article/alexander-hamilton/#3.

33 "Alexander Hamilton," New World Encyclopedia.

37 "Alexander Hamilton."

SELECTED BIBLIOGRAPHY

"Alexander Hamilton." New World Encyclopedia. https://www
.newworldencyclopedia.org/entry/Alexander_Hamilton.

Chernow, Ron. *Alexander Hamilton*. London: Penguin Books, 2004.

"Dueling." Encyclopedia.com.
https://www.encyclopedia.com/social-sciences-and-law/law/law
/dueling.

Kennedy, Lesley. "How Alexander Hamilton's Men Surprised the Enemy
at the Battle of Yorktown." History, November 14, 2018. https://www
.history.com/news/alexander-hamilton-battle-yorktown
-revolutionary-war.

Kiprop, Victor. "The Thirteen Colonies." *World Atlas*. https://www
.worldatlas.com/articles/the-thirteen-colonies.html.

O'Keefe, Kieran J. "Alexander Hamilton." George Washington's Mount
Vernon. https://www.mountvernon.org/library/digitalhistory/digital
-encyclopedia/article/alexander-hamilton/#3.

Randall, Willard Sterne. "Hamilton Takes Command." *Smithsonian*,
January 2003. https://www.smithsonianmag.com/history
/hamilton-takes-command-74722445/.

"10 Facts: Battle of Princeton." American Battlefield Trust. https://www
.battlefields.org/learn/articles/10-facts-battle-princeton.

Wallenfeldt, Jeffrey. "Whiskey Rebellion." *Encyclopedia Brittanica*.
https://www.britannica.com/event/Whiskey-Rebellion.

"Who Served Here? Alexander Hamilton." Independence Hall
Association. http://www.ushistory.org/valleyforge/served/hamilton
.html.

FURTHER READING

BOOKS

Castellano, Peter. *The American Revolution*. New York: Gareth Stevens, 2018. Dig into the history of the United States in this book about the American Revolution.

Kanefield, Teri. *Alexander Hamilton*. New York: Abrams Books for Young Readers, 2017. Learn more about Alexander Hamilton, a founder with radical ideas for the newly created United States.

Schwartz, Heather E. *Lin-Manuel Miranda: Revolutionary Playwright, Composer, and Actor*. Minneapolis: Lerner Publications, 2020. Read all about Lin-Manuel Miranda, writer of the hit musical *Hamilton*.

WEBSITES

Alexander Hamilton Facts for Kids
    https://kids.kiddle.co/Alexander_Hamilton
    Get the facts on Alexander Hamilton's life and legacy.

Founding Fathers
    https://kids.britannica.com/kids/article/Founding-Fathers/627390
    Who were the United States' founders? Find out here!

Revolutionary War
    https://www.history.com/topics/american-revolution/american
    -revolution-history
    Learn more about the American Revolution.

INDEX